Christian Marriage

*Bible Principles To Make God
The Foundation Of Your Christian Marriage*

Alexis G. Roldan

Copyright © 2017 by Alexis G. Roldan

All rights reserved. In no way is it legal to reproduce in whole or in part, duplicate, store in a retrieval system, or transmit this book in any form or by any means electronic, mechanical, or otherwise without written permission from the publisher.

The information provided herein is stated to be truthful and consistent, in that any liability, in terms of inattention or otherwise, by any usage or abuse of any policies, processes, or directions contained within is the sole responsibility of the recipient reader. Under no circumstances will any legal responsibility or blame be held against the publisher for any reparation, damages, or monetary loss due to the information herein, either directly or indirectly.

The information herein is offered for informational purposes solely, and is universal as so. The presentation of the information is without contract or any type of guarantee.

FREE BONUS MATERIAL

Christian Article Series

30 Articles That Will Enlighten Your Faith In God

(Over $27 Value)

For FREE access, go to:

StraightTalkOnLife.com/ChristianArticles

Table of Contents

Introduction - 3

Chapter 1: The Basic Step – Relationship With God - 5

Chapter 2: The Two Steps of Prayer and Bible Reading - 10

Chapter 3: The Rhythm of Communication - 14

Chapter 4: The Conflict Quickstep - 19

Chapter 5: The Foxtrot of Finances - 23

Chapter 6: The Sequences of Intimacy and Romance - 28

Chapter 7: The Circle of Children - 32

Chapter 8: Waltzing Through Household Duties and Chores - 39

Chapter 9: Balancing Marriage and Career - 43

Chapter 10: The Joy of Blessing Others - 47

Conclusion - 50

Introduction

Marriage is like a dance - a beautiful sequence of fluid movements as two people intertwine back and forth, sometimes touching, sometimes not. Every part of the body and soul is involved, as concentration is required to keep in time with the music. And of course it takes lots and lots of practice. It's the same with marriage, as two separate people learn to live together and share their lives with one another.

Sometimes the dance can flow smoothly and wonderfully, but other times there are painful collisions and bruised toes. But as the music continues to play, the dancers must get up and try again, and again, until they learn the intricate steps of the dance. Over time they will begin to feel more confident together as toes are stepped on less and less, until they come to a place of realizing that in fact they are gliding together more and more, enjoying the dance as it unfolds, and even learning new steps together.

In a Christian Marriage the dance is enhanced by the presence of Christ. As each partner focuses on God, taking their cues from Him, the dance becomes enthralling and exhilarating, especially because He is the one choosing the music. There may be difficult steps to learn, aching muscles and failures along the way, but through it all Jesus is the Master Choreographer who will teach His beloved ones how to succeed at the beautiful and magnificent Dance of Marriage.

This book will seek to discuss some of the 'dance steps' for life and for marriage which God has given us in His Word, the Bible. These are the foundations or principles for living a life that is pleasing to God and brings honor and glory to Him.

Each chapter will cover a particular aspect of married life, explaining what the Bible has to say about that aspect and how it can be applied within our marriages today. At the end of each chapter there will be some questions for reflection to help you think through the points that have been discussed.

Whether you are newly married or married for decades already, our prayer is that God will bring a refreshing perspective into your marriage. May you and your spouse take hold of the outstretched hands of Jesus as He invites you both to dance with Him. Let Him teach you the steps, and enjoy the dance together!

Chapter 1: The Basic Step – Relationship With God

Once upon a time, long long ago, in a beautiful garden called Eden, the very first wedding ceremony took place. Creator God Himself had lovingly formed the man and the woman, giving them to each other in marriage. And so the first dance of marriage began as the tantalizing strains of wedding music started to play while all of creation, the animals and the hosts of heaven looked on with fascination. But the couple were not left alone to figure out the steps together – their Father God, Master Choreographer was standing on the dance floor, waiting to teach them the basic steps, taking their hands and leading them on in relationship with Him.

In Relationship With God...

And so it is today, God is still the author and inventor of marriage. In the beginning when God created Adam from the dust, He saw that it was not good for the man to be alone. So God took one of Adam's ribs and created the first woman called Eve. When God presented Eve to Adam, they became man and wife in the presence of God (see Genesis 2: 7, 18, 21-23). Marriage was God's idea in the first place and He sees marriage as a good and wonderful relationship where husband and wife help each other to be the best that they can be. His presence within the marriage relationship gives the ultimate blessing, wisdom, guidance and protection. In order to have a Christian marriage, both husband and wife need to have committed their lives to Christ and have a living ongoing relationship with God.

In the Same Direction...

A wise person once said that love does not consist of gazing into one another's eyes but rather of looking together in the same direction. When both husband and wife are looking to God, they will be able to move forward together, and at the same time grow closer to one another as their relationship with God grows. This can also be illustrated by the triangle concept with God on top at the apex of the equilateral triangle and each spouse on either side of the base. As the couple move closer to God, they inevitably move closer to one another.

In Sync as Partners ...

Marriage is a partnership. When you are partners with someone you need to be able to work, play and live together harmoniously or in sync. The main, and in fact only non-negotiable requirement for being 'in sync' with someone is to share the same beliefs about God - in other words for both of you to be committed Christians. The Bible calls this fellowship – the fellowship of the spirit, when two or more people are like-minded, having the same love, being one in spirit and purpose (see Philippians 2:1-2).

Each one of us is totally unique and inevitably there will be scores of differences related to culture, personality, preferences and a million other things. And this is great – it's what makes a relationship exciting and fresh. But when it comes to your faith there needs to be unity in order for the 'dance' to flow with any kind of synchronization. There is a famous Bible verse relating to this where it says that we should not be yoked together, or unequally yoked, with unbelievers. The Message translation puts it this way: "Don't become partners with those who reject God. How can you make a partnership out of right and wrong? That's not a partnership; that's war. Is light best friends with dark? Does Christ go strolling with the Devil?" (see 1 Corinthians 6:14-16 The Message).

There are many difficult and heartbreaking instances where only one partner is a believer. Perhaps you married thinking that your souse would 'come around' to your way of faith, or perhaps you were under the impression that they were a committed Christian, only to discover after marriage that the commitment was not nearly as deep as yours... Either way, if you find yourself in a marriage where you are the only practicing Christian, the Apostle Peter's encouragement is to let the purity and reverence of your behavior be a testimony to draw your spouse's heart towards God (see 1 Peter 3:1-2). Nevertheless, this book will be speaking mainly to marriages where both partners are seeking to follow God.

In Exclusive Covenant ...

The marriage relationship is a covenant. This is a sacred agreement between two people in front of God. By definition it means that all others are excluded from the covenant. Hebrews 13:4 says: "Marriage should be honored by all, and the marriage bed kept pure, for God will judge the adulterer and all the sexually immoral." This means that when you get married your spouse becomes your one-and-only beloved, and you sever all ties with any previous partners you may have had. Faithfulness in marriage is the foundation for trust and respect, without which it is impossible to build a strong relationship. Through sexual intimacy in marriage, two people become "one flesh" (see Genesis 2:24). That is why unfaithfulness of either partner cause so much pain, devastation and heartaches as that union is ripped apart. God knows that when both husband and wife make a commitment from their hearts to be faithful and to love and cherish one another, their marriage will be blessed and go from strength to strength.

In it for Life...

Marriage was meant to last a lifetime. When God created marriage in the beginning He intended it to last until death (see Romans 7:2-3). Sadly however, due to sin and the hardness of people's hearts, divorce came into being (see Matthew 19:3-9). The reasons for dissolving a marriage are many and varied and every one of them includes severe pain, suffering and heartache. The verses saying that "God hates divorce" (Malachi 2:14-16) are widely known and quoted. In fact, what God really hates is the sin, strife, hatred, violence and unfaithfulness that inevitably accompany divorce. With His help it is possible to experience the loving, faithful and wonderful kind of marriage the way it was meant to be. This will still include a lot of hard work and ups and downs along the way as you learn to love and respect one another over time, but in the end it will be well worth the effort.

It Is All for God's Glory...

"...whatever you do, do it all for the glory of God." (1 Corinthians 10:31) This includes your marriage. The thing that brings the greatest glory to

God is when we become more and more like His Son Jesus Christ. Yes, Christlikeness is the main goal of every believer and every Christian couple. Christ came to earth not to be served but to serve (see Matthew 20:28) As we serve one another in marriage, and as the character or fruit of the Holy Spirit is developed more and more in our lives, (see Galatians 5:22-23) we will be bringing glory to God.

A Reflection of Christ and His Church...

Marriage is a reflection or a representation of Christ and the Church. The Bible tells us that the marriage relationship is a kind of symbol or a living example of the relationship between Christ and His Bride, the Church. Paul the Apostle explains this in his letter to the Ephesians (see Ephesians 5:22-32). In fact he describes it as a profound mystery. Therefore we can understand that the love between a husband and wife who are living their lives in a good relationship with God and with one another is somehow a representation of the love that Jesus Christ has for His people. It is a sacrificial and unselfish love that is willing to put the needs of the other person first. This kind of love is also patient and kind. "It does not envy, it does not boast, it is not proud... It always protects, always trusts, always hopes, always perseveres... Love never fails." (1Corinthians 13:4-8)

Questions for Reflection:

- Are you a child of God and do you and your spouse have a relationship with Him?
- If so, how can you encourage and support one another as you seek to keep Christ at the center of your marriage.
- If you are not sure about your relationship with God, or if you would like to re-commit your life to Him, you may want to use this prayer as a guideline:

Dear God, I know that I am a sinner in need of a Savior. I choose to repent and turn away from my sins. Please will you forgive me? Thank You Jesus, for dying on the cross in my place, and for rising from the dead so that I too can have everlasting life. Please will You be my Lord and Savior. I hand over every area of my life to You, including my marriage. Please will You come and teach me the right steps in this dance of marriage. Please fill me with Your Holy Spirit so that I can live for You day by day. Amen.

Chapter 2: The Two Steps of Prayer and Bible Reading

Now that we have established the first basic step of having a relationship with God , it's time to learn the next movements and sequences that make up the practical expression of that relationship. There are two steps in particular which can have a truly profound effect in your marriage relationship and that is praying and reading the Bible together. When you make a regular habit of reading God's word and joining hands together in prayer, you will find that your spiritual intimacy will grow. Just as physical intimacy is important (see chapter six), so is emotional, mental and spiritual intimacy. Remember that God is your Master Choreographer and He wants to share with you and teach you – so in order for that to happen, you need to be in touch and listening for His voice. Prayer is simply a conversation which consists of speaking and listening on the part of all concerned.

Prayer is a Conversation...

Some people are more talkative than others, but when you are in a relationship with someone you love, then talking is inevitable. Do you remember when you and your spouse were first getting to know one another, how the hours seemed to fly? It was as if there were not enough hours in the day for everything you wanted to say to each other. As the years go by, you may reach a stage where you feel there is not much left to talk about except the superficial day to day events of your life. But with God there is always something new and fresh. His mercies are new every morning (Lamentations 3:22-23) and He is doing new things in our lives all the time (Isaiah 43:19). When we include Him in the conversation, or rather let Him direct the conversation, it is sure to be a good one.

Prayer is Spontaneous as Well as Planned...

So if prayer is a conversation, should it happen spontaneously and randomly, or should it be structured and planned? The best answer is probably a combination of these approaches, and every couple needs to find their own rhythm of what works well in their particular situation. Just as it is good to cultivate the habit of regular prayer at certain times, it is also great to be able to pray freely and openly at any time. Here are a few suggestions which can be helpful in practicing your prayer life together:

- When you wake up in the morning, spend some time thanking God for the night that has passed and the new day ahead. Share with each other your prayer requests and then pray specifically for God's wisdom and protection for whatever you are facing. Also pray for your children and families.
- In the evening before you go to sleep, take time to thank God for His help and intervention that day and commit each other to God again for the night.
- At any time throughout the day or night when you feel the need, you can take your spouse's hand and say, "Let's pray" – whether it's a child that is struggling, an upsetting phone call from a friend, or a development on the news. Any time is the right time to pray.
- Whenever there is some special occasion in your family, such as a birthday or anniversary, remember to pray for that person, thanking God for their life and praying His blessing over them.

Although you can pray continuously and silently in your hearts as individuals, what a privilege it is to be able to pray together with your beloved. As God says, when two or three gather in His name He is there and when two agree it will be done (Matthew 18:19-20).

Besides the privilege of praying together, the other significant part of the two-step is reading the Bible together. Have you ever wished that married life came with some kind of 'manual'? Well, that is why God gave us the Bible!

The Bible is God's Manual for Life- Including Marriage...

Life is full of ups and downs with challenges and pitfalls at every turn and it is easy to get caught up in the rush and bustle of our daily lives. If we don't take the time to draw aside regularly and read God's word, listening for His Holy Spirit in our hearts speaking into our situation, then we can end up feeling like we are on the hamster wheel – going round and round in circles.

Although the Bible was written centuries ago, it is still the most up to date document in terms of wisdom and insight for every situation we may face, especially in marriage. If you are not already in the habit of regular Bible reading, then it may seem like a daunting prospect to begin. Or perhaps you and your spouse read your Bibles individually, but not usually together. Why not try something new now, and see what God will do in your relationship? Here are a few thoughts and suggestions to get you going as you read the Bible together:

- Start with one of the shorter books – like Mark's Gospel, Colossians or Esther. Then when you have finished that book you can move on to another one.
- Remember it is not a competition or a contest, and quality is always more important than quantity. When you are reading and something stands out for you, stop and discuss it. Or if you don't understand a certain passage, do some research and ask God to explain it to you.
- Take turns to read aloud to each other. You could also do this while you are travelling in the car, or while you are waiting for an appointment.
- Maybe you would like to use a good devotional book which highlights a daily Bible passage and then gives a commentary.
- Try to memorize your favorite verses or write them out on cards so you can remind each other or read them out to each other.
- Find passages that are appropriate for difficult times and read them out aloud together as a declaration in the spiritual realm. God's word spoken aloud is a powerful weapon against Satan, the enemy of our souls. One example of a good passage to read aloud is Isaiah 43:1-3

"... This is what the LORD says – He who created you... He who formed you... 'Fear not, for I have redeemed you; I have summoned you by name; you are mine. When you pass through the waters, I will be with you; and when you pass through the rivers, they will not sweep over you. When you walk through fire, you will not be burned; the flames will not set you ablaze. For I am the LORD, your God, the Holy One of Israel, your Savior..."

Try to have a regular time when you read the Bible together every day, perhaps in the morning or at night. Or maybe you can only manage it once or twice a week – don't be discouraged. Remember God is not legalistic and He is always there for you, waiting to speak to you. The more you do it the more you will begin to see how relevant God's word is for your life and how He seems to pinpoint exactly the right verse on the exact day when you need it.

Questions for Reflection:
- Do you and your spouse have regular times when you pray and read the Bible together?
- Do you feel free to pray aloud with your spouse? If not, what is holding you back and how can you address this?
- How can you and your spouse encourage one another to be more intentional about making the time for these two vital steps of prayer and Bible reading?

Chapter 3: The Rhythm of Communication

Without communication there can be no relationship at all. In fact, communication is what it is all about in marriage – the better you can communicate, the better and more satisfying your relationship will be. Thankfully communication is a skill that can be learned and worked on and improved. So if you feel that you are not naturally a good communicator, you are in great company, because to some extent it is something we all have to spend our whole lives learning.

God is the Master Communicator, and He has been communicating and reaching out to His people since the beginning of time. In fact Jesus Himself is called The Word! (John 1:1). God sent His Son Jesus into the world to teach us (John 7:16) and when Jesus returned to heaven He sent the Holy Spirit to teach us (John 14:16). Ultimately God speaks to us through His word in the Bible, which thoroughly equips us for every good work (2 Timothy 3:16-17).

In the context of marriage, communication is especially powerful because our words can be used to either build up or break down our spouse. Proverbs 18:21 says that the tongue has the power of life and death, and those who love it will eat its fruit. This chapter will consider some biblical principles and pointers which can help us to develop a positive and productive rhythm of communication in our marriage, as well as highlighting some of the pitfalls to avoid.

Communicating both verbally and non-verbally...

How many of you know that it is possible to communicate a great deal without saying one word? The minute your spouse walks through the door you can know if it's been a good day or a bad day. Either they are frowning and tense, or they are smiling and relaxed. Yes, body language can constitute between sixty to ninety percent of all communication. This includes things like facial expressions, whether or not eye contact is made, and the tone of voice that is used, as well as body postures such as folded arms and legs.

So remember, when you are communicating face to face with your loved one, the words you say are only a small part of the message you are giving. If you want to communicate authentically, your words need to be matched by your tone and body language. In order to foster loving and open communication, you need to make eye contact and have an open posture towards your spouse. It's no use saying, "Tell me what is wrong, I want to understand and help..." when you have your arms folded defensively, you do not look your spouse in the eye, and your tone is one of frustration and irritation. This creates dissonance and the end result is that your spoken words are perceived as being untrustworthy.

Getting to know each other...

The longer you live with someone, the more you will get to know what they are like, what makes them happy or sad, what kind of situations they find relaxing or stressful, and what makes them angry or excited. This kind of knowledge comes through spending time together, but it does not automatically happen; you need to be intentional in seeking to notice and understand what kind of person your spouse is. It's an exciting adventure – somewhat like a treasure hunt, where every little clue along the way will take you a step closer to winning the heart of your beloved.

When we really take time to get to know our spouse, the rewards are priceless. A husband or wife who feels known and understood by their beloved will be able to trust and confide on a deeper level. The Bible says in 1 Peter 3:7 that husbands should live with their wives 'according to knowledge...' (KJV) and this certainly applies to wives as well. The more we know each other the better we will be able to communicate effectively.

Learning to listen well...

"You're not listening to me!" is a cry of frustration which is often heard in the home. Why is it so difficult for us to really listen? The Bible says 'everyone should be quick to listen, slow to speak and slow to become angry' (James 1:19). Keeping quiet while the other one is speaking is a prerequisite to effective listening, but listening is more than just keeping quiet – it requires paying careful attention and focusing on the other person. Sometimes it means switching off the TV, putting down the cell phone or newspaper, turning towards your spouse and looking into their eyes while they speak.

The degree to which we listen to someone can be quite an accurate measure of how much we love that person. Loving listening is actually the foundation for good communication. When you listen properly and sensitively to your spouse they will be much more likely and willing to listen to you in return. Often there is a lot of talking and arguing going on with not much listening taking place. This is when it can be very helpful to draw back and practice just keeping quiet and trying to hear what is really taking place. In Proverbs 10:19 we are told that 'When words are many, sin is not absent, but he who holds his tongue is wise.'

For a Christian couple seeking to honor God in their relationship, it is of primary importance for both to be listening not only to each other but especially to God's Holy Spirit. God says: 'Listen, listen to Me, and eat what is good, and your soul will delight in the richest of fare. Give ear and come to Me; hear Me, that your soul may live.' (Isaiah 55:2-3)

Being mindful of gender differences...

A lot of misunderstandings and miscommunications occur because husbands and wives fail to recognize that essentially men and women are quite different. These differences are both physical and emotional which results in different ways of communicating. When you expect your spouse to say and do things exactly the same way as you do, there are bound to be disappointments. God created man and woman differently, so that they could complement and help one another, while both of them together reflect His image (see Genesis 1:27).

Women generally tend to be more emotional and sensitive while men are more goal oriented. When a wife is sharing her heart with her husband, often she is looking only for a listening ear, comfort, acceptance and affirmation – not a logical solution to all her 'problems.'

On the other hand, when the husband starts to speak, he would need and appreciate focused silence, without any interruptions or 'affirmations' until he has finished and then is ready to receive some feedback.

God calls us to honor and respect the differences between genders rather than being resentful or trying to change each other (see 1 Peter 3:7). Husbands and wives need to learn from one another, honoring their differences and helping each other to feel accepted for who God has uniquely made them to be, and in the process this will greatly enhance the communication between them.

Avoiding the pitfalls...

They say prevention is better than cure and this is certainly true for communication. There are some common communication mistakes or pitfalls which can cause havoc in a marriage relationship. If you recognize any of these in your marriage, please take the necessary steps to deal with them before your relationship is completely compromised. These dangerous pitfalls include:

- Shouting, yelling or screaming: raising your voice and freely venting your anger can unfortunately become an easy habit. The Bible says that 'a fool gives full vent to his anger, but a wise man keeps himself under control' (Proverbs 29:11).
- Stonewalling: This is the opposite of yelling, when one or both partners simply refuse to speak to each other. This is a favorite method of passive aggression used by those who seek to punish, control, dominate and intimidate their spouse. This is completely contrary to God's way which says that if you have something against someone you should speak it out with them (see Matthew 18: 15-17)
- Having topics which are taboo: If there are touchy subjects which you and your spouse refuse to discuss, this can be seen as a red flag which prevents intimacy on a heart to heart level. Even if the subject is painful and embarrassing, over time, with patience and

God's wisdom and grace, it is possible to have no 'off-limit' areas in your relationship.
- Competiveness: God created husband and wife to complete each other, not to compete with each other. When marriage becomes a competition to see who is the best, quickest, cleverest or highest earner, then you are missing the point altogether.
- Selfishness: 'Do nothing out of selfish ambition or vain conceit, but in humility consider others better than yourselves' (Philippians 2:3). A Godly marriage is about serving your spouse and seeking what is best for them.
- Pride: Being proud means not being willing to admit when you are wrong. If only one partner in a marriage is always the one doing the apologizing and asking forgiveness while the other partner never acknowledges doing anything wrong, this is a huge imbalance and is probably indicative of some abnormality such as emotional abuse. God opposes and resists the proud (James 4:6).

Questions for Reflection:
- How would you rate your communication with your spouse on a scale of one to ten?
- Do you feel that your spouse listens to you attentively, and vice versa?
- What can you do to improve the rhythm of communicate between you and your spouse?
- Do you recognize any of the communication 'pitfalls' in your marriage relationship? If so, what can you do to address these issues? If you are not able to see any improvement within a reasonable time, please consider finding a Christian counsellor or pastor to help you overcome these areas according to God's standards.

Chapter 4: The Conflict Quickstep

Just as the quickstep dance involves a lot of fast and powerful movements, so too does conflict in marriage. When it comes to resolving conflicts, sometimes a lot of fancy footwork is required, leaving both parties spinning wildly. And if you are not careful, the slightest slip or careless word can take you reeling way off course. Speaking of 'quicksteps', it is vital in a Christian marriage that steps are taken quickly to resolve any disputes and anger, otherwise our enemy Satan is able to gain ground in our lives and undermine our relationship with God and our spouse. As the Apostle Paul says in Ephesians 4:26-27 "In your anger do not sin; do not let the sun go down while you are still angry, and do not give the devil a foothold." Whether we like to admit it or not, every marriage relationship will involve some degree of conflict – even healthy marriages.

Conflict is normal in a close relationship...

Think about the fact that two completely separate and unique individuals with different personalities, different backgrounds and different needs, have now decided to blend their lives in this adventure called marriage. Some sparks of disagreement and conflict are surely inevitable. Sooner or later you will probably offend and irritate each other as you face the day to day stresses and challenges of life. So don't despair if there is conflict in your marriage – know that it is normal and with God's help you can learn to handle it effectively together. In fact, conflicts that are handled well tend to draw you closer to one another.

Zero conflict is not always a good sign...

Actually, if there is very little or no conflict in a marriage relationship, it probably means that one partner (or even both) is not being honest and is suppressing their own personality in order to keep the peace at any price. This is a very high price to pay and it does not result in a healthy marriage. On the contrary, it is healthier to accept that conflicts are a fact of life, and that in themselves, conflicts are not destructive. However, the way you handle your conflicts is what will determine how destructive or constructive they are.

How to handle conflicts...

The way you chose to handle the conflicts in your marriage will have one of two results; either it will drive a wedge between you and cause isolation, or it will strengthen your love and bring you closer to one another. The following pointers will help you to move in the direction of the latter outcome, namely reconciliation and greater intimacy.

- **Include God in your conflicts**

Remember God is your Master Choreographer, and when things go wrong on the dance floor He is the One who can help you. One of the biggest mistakes you can make is to think "Well, we have messed up now, so we had better sort it out somehow by ourselves" and you exclude God from the process, thinking He is away on the side somewhere folding His arms and waiting for you to get back on track... This is exactly what your enemy Satan wants you to think. No – God is right there, very much involved and looking with love and concern at every move you make and every word you say. So rather look to Him quickly, pray and ask for His help and wisdom as you seek to settle your differences in a way that will be pleasing to Him, according to His ways.

- **Honesty is essential**

Both of you need to be fully committed to be completely honest with each other and also with yourself. When your spouse senses that there is something bothering you and asks, "What's wrong, Honey?" it is not helpful to say "nothing" when there obviously is something wrong. The longer you stuff things down and deny your real feelings, the worse they will become. Then one day when the pressure builds up too much, there might be a nasty explosion which causes much more damage than if you had just expressed your concerns right up front. Honesty means being open and transparent to the point of painful vulnerability. But honesty must also be balanced with love, sharing your feelings clearly without condemning or blaming. Ephesians 4:15 says that we should speak the truth in love, so that we will grow up into Christ.

- **It is more than 50-50**

A healthy relationship cannot be built on a 50-50 arrangement or philosophy. In a Christian marriage each partner needs to be one hundred percent committed to the relationship which means being willing to go beyond halfway to help and support each other when needed. The kind of love described in 1 Corinthians 13:4-7 is what will carry you through, especially when there are conflicts to resolve. This kind of love does not keep scores and does not even think about who is giving the most. Incidentally, it is essential that both partners come to the party – if only one is always giving hundred percent while the other just takes and demands, the relationship will eventually break down.

- **Express feelings appropriately**

As discussed in the previous chapter on communication, body language and non-verbal factors play a huge part in how we express ourselves. Some of these can be very destructive and unhelpful when you are trying to resolve a conflict, for example yelling and screaming, or slamming doors and throwing things around. On the other end of the spectrum, silence, denial and stonewalling are equally counter-productive. If feelings are running high it is better to take a cooling off time and then come back later and talk things through when you are able to do so calmly. Try getting alone and venting your feelings to the LORD first – He is big enough to handle your temper without being hurt. Then when you sit down with your spouse you can express your feelings appropriately, using clear and honest words. If you are angry, frustrated or disappointed, talk about your feelings using "I" statements (e.g. I feel sad) rather than "you" statements (e.g. You make me sad).

- **Use the three step approach**

When something has happened and you need to confront your spouse, it is helpful to follow this simple rubric so that you can stay on track and not get drawn into side issues:

- State exactly what happened: Example: "My Darling, yesterday I was looking forward to going shopping with you after work as we

had planned. Then you changed your mind at the last minute because you wanted to stay home and watch TV."
- Explain how you were affected: "I was disappointed because I had been looking forward to it all day. Our children were also affected because I had arranged for them to go to their cousin's house while we were out."
- Say how you would have liked the situation to be handled: "I would have liked you to tell me earlier in the day that you did not want to go, not at the last minute, and to reschedule another time when you will be available."

- **Forgiveness is key**

The only way to successfully overcome conflicts is to forgive. This brings comfort and healing so that you can be reconciled and carry on with renewed strength and a deeper intimacy with your beloved. Forgiveness means giving up resentments and the desire to punish or get even. By an act of your will you decide to let the other person off your hook and start on a clean page with them. When both husband and wife can ask for forgiveness and grant forgiveness to each other quickly and willingly, the beautiful dance of marriage can proceed gracefully. God's word says that we should be kind and compassionate to one another, forgiving each other, just as in Christ God forgave us (Ephesians 4:32).

Questions for Reflection:
- Do you see conflict as a "normal" part of your marriage or do you think of every conflict as some kind of "failure".
- Think of the most recent conflict between you and your spouse – was it successfully resolved? If not, can you think of something you could have done differently?
- What is the one point from this chapter which stood out the most for you?

Chapter 5: The Foxtrot of Finances

Well, there is no prize for knowing that finances are one of the biggest problem areas in marriages. This part of the marriage dance can sometimes seem like the foxtrot rhythm which goes slow, slow, quick, quick... when the finances come in slow, slow and they leave quick, quick! Yes, managing the finances can seem like a maze or a minefield at times, but the real question is "How does God want us to handle our money?" The answer to this question will be the subject of this chapter, as we explore some of the things that the Bible says about finances, and how this can be applied within the marriage relationship.

Everything comes from God anyway...

Psalm 24:1 tells us that "the earth is the LORD'S, and everything in it, the world, and all who live in it. Then in 1 Chronicles 29:10-20 we read the beautiful prayer of David when the people brought their gifts for building the temple. David says, "Praise be to You, O LORD, God of our father Israel, from everlasting to everlasting. Yours, O LORD is the greatness and the power and the glory and the majesty and the splendor, for everything in heaven and earth is yours... wealth and honor come from You." Then David goes on to express how privileged he and the people felt to be able to give to God, saying that "everything comes from You and we have given You only what comes from Your hand." So although we can talk about "our" money, it is important to remember that in fact it is not ours to own but rather it is only ours in the sense that we are responsible to manage it and use it for God's glory.

Give to God first...

Our God is very generous and He gives us everything we need and more. One of the wonderful promises in the Bible is that "you will be made rich in every way so that you can be generous on every occasion" (2 Corinthians 9:11). When it comes to tithing or giving ten percent of your income to God, we read in Leviticus 27:30 that the tithe is holy and it belongs to God. Tithing is one of those good habits which help to keep us from becoming totally self-centered and selfish. Giving at least ten percent of your income to your church or charity of your choice, gives you a certain sense of satisfaction which comes from knowing that you have in some way given a lift to someone else's burden. Perhaps you feel you can't afford a tithe, but you can still afford to give in kind, whether it's your time, or generous hospitality. Both of you should be in agreement about this and be able to give willingly and cheerfully. They say, no one is ever too poor to give, and no one is ever so rich that they don't need anything in life.

The Debt Dilemma...

The big "D" word can be extremely difficult to cope with, especially if you are newly married. Debt can slowly strangle and drain the strength out of any marriage. The Bible says that we should let no debt remain outstanding, except the continuing debt to love one another (Romans 13:8). Firstly you need to be completely honest about all your outstanding debts. Don't deny or brush aside the ones you can't face as they will only grow and make things worse in the end. Face your debts together and if necessary get help in working out a repayment plan. Debt counselling is widely available and there is a way forward in every situation. Once you are able to reach a debt-free status, do everything you can as a couple to stay out of debt as much as possible.

Some Do's and Don'ts...

The following Do's and Don'ts will highlight some helpful aspects and suggestions for handling your finances as a married couple

- **DO: Work as a team**

  Teamwork applies not only to your finances but also to every area of your marriage relationship. You need to think about whether you will keep separate accounts, or pool all your finances. Do you still have a mentality of 'mine' and 'yours', or do you think in terms of 'ours'? Competitiveness can be a real obstacle to working as a team. If you feel that somehow you have to compete and constantly prove yourself to your mate, it will prevent you from seeing what is best for both of you together.

- **DO: Make a Budget**
  Although the experts agree that making a budget is the best way to handle your finances efficiently, it is surprising how few couples actually do this. Do yourselves a favor and take the time and effort to sit down and put together a budget. Remember to pray and ask God for His wisdom as you do this. Once you see exactly what income you have, and what your expenses are, then you can decide how to allocate your available funds. When you avoid the mistake of not making a budget, you will find you discover a certain freedom from constant concern and uncertainty which will be well worth the effort. Setting up a marriage budget can also be a great opportunity to get to know each other on a deeper level. As you thrash out the nitty-gritty of your monthly, weekly and daily expenses, you can decide together what is essential, what is important and what is not so important or even disposable. If you have never kept a budget before, this is a great time to start. It will no doubt be a learning curve for both of you and give you a set of boundaries which helps to give you peace of mind, knowing you will make it financially, if you stay within the budget you have agreed on together.

- **DO: Discuss your financial goals**
  As a married couple you probably have several goals together, as well as some individual goals. When it comes to your financial goals, it is best if you are pulling together in the same direction. Sit down, discuss and come to an agreement on what you are saving up towards, whether it is buying a new car, building your own home one day, or sending your children to the best schools. This way you can keep each other motivated and accountable, and you are much more likely to accomplish your goals together. It is good to discuss and pray through these questions regularly as you re-evaluate your financial goals from time to time, as the seasons of your life progress.

- **DON'T: Have Secrets**
  Playing open cards is always the best policy in marriage when it comes to expenses, or anything else for that matter. If this is not your first marriage and you have alimony and child support to pay, your new future wife deserves to know that up front. And if you have any outstanding loans or credit accounts, these should also be put on the table. Nothing breaks trust in a marriage as quickly as finding out that your partner lied to you, or deliberately hid something important from you. So remember, one of the best money and marriage tips is to avoid keeping secrets about expenses.

- **DON'T: Argue**
  Another mistake which wears a couple down is constant bickering and arguing about finances. Arguing seldom accomplishes anything constructive. It better to stop yourselves in your tracks, nip arguing in the bud, and find some positive solutions to your money problems. Agree on a strategy that you will implement together, and agree to talk about things sensibly, without arguing, blaming or complaining. Philippians 2:14 says that we should do everything without complaining or arguing.

- **DON'T: Use Power Plays**
  Avoid using money to manipulate, punish or control your spouse in any way. This is called financial abuse. It is particularly applicable if one spouse is the breadwinner whilst the other stays home taking care of the kids. The malignant misconception often occurs where the one earning the salary feels that he is the only one 'working'. Even if both are working, in a healthy marriage there should not be the concept of 'my' money, but rather 'ours'.

Finally, when it comes to navigating the foxtrots of marriage finances, our goal should be to reach a place of contentment, knowing that God is our provider and he will give us everything we need to do His will. The Apostle Paul says it well in Philippians 4:11-13 "... I have learned to be content whatever the circumstances. I know what it is to be in need, and I know what it is to have plenty. I have learned the secret of being content in any and every situation, whether well fed or hungry, whether living in plenty or in want. I can do everything through Him who gives me strength."

Questions for Reflection:
- To what extent are financial issues a struggle for you and your spouse?
- Which of the Do's and Don'ts would you like to work on in your marriage? What ways can you think of to make an improvement in this area?
- Do you feel that you can say with the Apostle Paul: "I have learned to be content..." If not, ask God to help you and give you His peace regarding your finances.

Chapter 6: The Sequences of Intimacy and Romance

God created marriage to be romantic and joyful. According to the Bible, the marriage relationship is meant to be full of romance, physical attraction, excitement and pure joy. One entire book of the Bible is written in the form of a play or drama between two passionate lovers, namely Solomon and his Beloved Shulamite . (Read Song of Songs) The eight chapters of this book describe, in beautiful poetical language, their love for one another and the way they find each other's bodies attractive and irresistible! For example, Solomon says to his bride: "Your two breasts are like two fawns, like twin fawns of a gazelle that browse among the lilies." (Song of Songs 4:5) And later on she says of him: "His arms are rods of gold set with chrysolite. His body is like polished ivory decorated with sapphires." (Song of Songs 5:14)

Another great love story in the Old Testament is between Jacob and Rachel. In fact he was willing to work seven years for her father before he was allowed to marry her. Genesis 29:20 says: "So Jacob served seven years to get Rachel, but they seemed like only a few days to him because of his love for her." And then we have the exciting romance of Ruth and Boaz, not to mention David and Abigail, Esther and King Xerxes and many more. The Bible is full of love stories, and ultimately the greatest love story of all is the sacred romance between God and His people: "For God so loved the world that He gave His one and only Son, that whoever believes in him shall not perish but have eternal life" (John 3:16).

When you hear the word "romance" do you think only of dating couples or newlyweds? What about couples who have been married for a year or two, or five, ten, twenty or more years? Although the years can bring about many changes in a couple's relationship, it is still very possible to keep the romance alive and well, to the point that you become in fact more and more "in love" with each other as the years go by. But this is by no means an automatic process – it requires conscious and continuous effort on the part of both spouses whilst continually trusting God and allowing Him to be the focal point of your intimacy and romance.

Perhaps you have become aware that things have gotten a bit "stale" in your marriage and maybe you're just so busy and exhausted by the time you flop into bed at night. The fact that you have realized this is good if you take it as a wakeup call. Now is a great time to start doing those little things which can make a big difference. There are many different ways to keep the romance alive in your marriage every day as each couple has unique preferences and favorites. Below are some ideas and suggestions to help you along on the exciting journey of keeping your marriage relationship close, contended and creative. As you practice and learn the sequences of intimacy and romance, remember that God is your Master Choreographer who knows all the best and most exciting steps.

Make Hello's and Goodbye's Count...

Simple but thoughtful greetings can go a long way to keeping the romance alive in your marriage and setting a good tone for the day. As you say good bye when you leave for work, instead of rushing off with a quick peck on the cheek and a hasty "see you later", take just a few seconds longer for a real kiss and a loving word. Tell your spouse that you will be thinking of them while you are apart and you will look forward to seeing them again. As they leave, watch them drive (or walk) away until they are out of sight and give a final wave when they are about to disappear. And then when you come home again after work, instead of a casual "Hi, how was your day?" make it a mini reunion. Give each other a smile, a hug and a nice long kiss that really says, "I missed you and I'm so glad to see you again."

Be Thankful for Every Blessing...

Being thankful can be the single most effective antidote to a whole range of negative emotions such as depression, anxiety, complaining and arguing. If we can just recognize and focus on how blessed we are, it makes all our challenges easier to bear. Don't take anything about your spouse for granted. The fact that they married you is the first thing to be grateful for. Then there are countless things which you can make a point of thanking your spouse for specifically everyday – for cooking a meal, washing your clothes, helping the kids with schoolwork, fixing the leaking faucet, mowing the lawn, or any other practical thing they may have done. And don't forget be thankful to your spouse for things like being a good listener, a faithful friend and a loving parent to your children. And most of all, remember to thank God for all His blessings to you every day: "So then, just as you received Christ Jesus as LORD, continue to live in Him, rooted and built up in Him, strengthened in the faith as you were taught, and overflowing with thankfulness."(Colossians 2:6-7)

Help Around the House...

Sometimes the most romantic thing you can do for your spouse is to hang out a load of washing, load the dishwasher, or wash the windows. Cooking a meal together is very romantic too and of course nothing beats taking turns to change baby diapers! Don't expect your spouse to feel intimate and romantic if she is exhausted from doing all the chores around the house while you relax watching TV every evening until bedtime. When you show some consideration and willingness to help, you may just be surprised to find how the flame of romance is ignited in your marriage. And as you get through the chores quicker together you will have more time to relax and enjoy one another's company every day.

Brag About Each Other...

It's one thing to compliment your spouse in private when it's just the two of you – and that is very good and important – but it is also great when you say good things about each other in public. Whether it's on social media, at the office or when you are out with friends, and especially with your children. Take every opportunity to brag about each other, in a sincere way, to let your friends, families and colleagues know that you think your spouse is the greatest. And don't do it only when your spouse is listening, but also do it behind their back – expressing your appreciation and thankfulness for the person you chose to marry.

Use Any Excuse to Celebrate...

Your marriage is certainly something worth celebrating, but don't just wait for your anniversary or Valentine's Day. Find any and every reason to celebrate, whether it's a first-kiss date, engagement date or any other random calendar date. Get out the candles, balloons and cake, invite some special friends and family over, or make a romantic table setting just for the two of you. Remembering and cherishing special events is a great way to build your own family traditions and set a strong and secure foundation of blessing and trust in your marriage.

Once you get into the swing of practicing these ways to keep romance and intimacy alive in your marriage every day you may just find that you start coming up with lots more ideas of your own, as you go from strength to strength in your relationship with God and with your spouse.

Questions for Reflection:
- Do you feel that intimacy and romance are still alive and well in your marriage? Or could it be better? Or do you need some serious resuscitation?
- Depending on how you answered the first question, which of the suggestions above would you like to start working on with your spouse?
- What other ideas and suggestions do you have to keep the intimacy and romance in your marriage alive and growing?

Chapter 7: The Circle of Children

Marriage is the best setting to raise a family. Children are one of the many blessings of marriage. God blessed Adam and Eve and told them to be fruitful and multiply (Genesis 1:28). A marriage between two people who love God and love each other is the ideal setting in which to raise a healthy family. The Bible says that we are to train up our children and teach them the right way to live (Proverbs 22:6). Children are to obey their parents, and parents should bring them up lovingly in the instruction of the Lord without exasperating and provoking them (see Ephesians 6:1-4)

When the pitter-patter of little feet begin to join your circle in the dance of marriage there is inevitably a change of pace and rhythm. Lots of new steps need to be learned and there are huge adjustments to be made as you both get used to the new dynamic of parenthood. As always, your Master Choreographer, Father God is right there with you to teach you and help you through the exciting years of bringing up the precious children that He has blessed you with. Psalm 127 tells us that children are a heritage from the LORD and a reward, like arrows in the hand of a warrior. "Blessed is the man whose quiver is full of them." (Psalm 127:3-5)

Parenthood – a terrifying privilege...

Becoming a parent can be the most wonderful and terrifying experience of your life. Perhaps you've been looking forward to this for many years, or perhaps it's the last thing you expected to happen to you! Whatever your expectation was, you are bound to be in for a few surprises along the way. At some or other point you may just find yourself thinking, "I wasn't prepared for this" and "I wish there was some kind of handbook!" Well, the good news is that although your baby is not delivered with a personalized handbook, there is indeed a lot of help available, especially in the Bible.

Parenting requires being conscious and mindful...

If we are open and willing to learn, parenthood can be the most exhilarating growth experience ever. There are countless sources from which we can learn: from others who have gone before us; from our own experiences; and most definitely from our children who often prove to be our greatest "teachers" in so many ways. Conscious parenting is all about being deliberate and thoughtful in what we do as parents, being aware of our child's needs as well as our own needs as changes and progress take place. The Bible tells us that we should be self-controlled and alert (that is conscious and mindful) because our enemy Satan is prowling around like a roaring lion looking for someone to devour (1 Peter 5:8). This is certainly true where parenthood is concerned.

The following discussion of conscious parenting will outline six pertinent aspects that you need to be conscious of as you seek to bring up your children in Godly ways so that they will learn to know and love God for themselves.

- **Be conscious of your own history**
  Whatever you have experienced in your own childhood will have a definite impact on the kind of parent you become one day. It is important to face your past squarely and if necessary get help to deal with whatever pain or trauma you may have gone through. Every one of us will pick up some or other wounds along the way, no matter how great our parents were, there will always be some struggles. Sometimes we try to stuff down and deny the things that have hurt us in the past, bravely moving on, perhaps even vowing that when we become a parent we will never be like our own parents... Unfortunately, sooner or later these things will pop up again, until we can reach a place of acceptance, forgiveness, healing and peace with the help of God's Holy Spirit.

- **Be conscious of spiritual meaning in your life**
  Parenthood is a very sacred experience – when you witness the miracle of bringing forth a brand new life into this world, you realize that there is so much more to life than what meets the eye. Being

conscious of spiritual meaning in your life is important at any time, and especially when you become responsible for a child, you need to know what you will teach that child about life, about God and about spiritual matters. As a Christian couple, you need to decide together how you are going to teach your children, and the structures you will put in place for their spiritual nurture, including things like Bible reading, prayer and church attendance. In Deuteronomy 6:6-7 God says that His words are to be upon our hearts; "Impress them on your children. Talk about them when you sit at home and when you walk along the road, when you lie down and when you get up." Finding the spiritual meaning in your life will give you the strength and guidance you will need to face the awesome and awe-inspiring adventure of parenting.

- **Be conscious of your reasons and motives for having a child**
Conscious parenting includes the momentous decision to have a child in the first place. Naturally there can be many reasons and motives for wanting a family, and ideally these should be about the child rather than the adult. In fact, the only really relevant reason for having a child is the desire to love and cherish, to provide for, teach and prepare another person to reach maturity and be a benefit to society and most importantly a Christian who honors God with their life. If these are not your reasons then perhaps you need to wait a while until you can be prepared to have the best interests of your child at heart, knowing that you are willing and able to give your child whatever they will need to reach adulthood in a healthy way. If you are already a parent, ask God to bring your motives and attitudes towards your children into line with His Godly order.

- **Be conscious of every stage of parenthood**
Children grow up so quickly! Before you know it that cute little bundle of joy is starting to talk and walk, and then it's off to school and soon you will have a teenager in your home! Part of conscious parenting is to savor and cherish every stage and phase of your child's life, whether it's teething, or getting braces, learning to ride a

bicycle, or getting a driver's license. Every stage can be precious and full of memories which will enrich the years to come for both you and your child. So make the years count and collect the memories to bring out and enjoy on a rainy day.

- **Be conscious of our own faults and mistakes**
  None of us is perfect and if you didn't know it already, you will find out soon enough when you become a parent. In some cultures and families there is a very harmful belief that the parent should never say sorry to the child – that this will cause the child to lose respect for the adult. On the contrary, a parent who can be open about their own faults, weaknesses and mistakes is teaching their child an extremely valuable life lesson in humbleness and integrity. Asking forgiveness of one another is essential to a healthy and happy home.

- **Be conscious of mentoring the next generation**
  Being a mentor involves modelling good values and behavior, firstly to our own children and then also to others in the next generation. Sadly, many young people today do not have parents who are involved in their lives, but thankfully there are older men and women who are willing to step up and make a significant difference by actively and consciously parenting and mentoring children who are not their own. Every one of us has a responsibility to help shape and mentor the next generation, whether we are parents or not.

Parenting Requires Skill...
Besides the aspects described above that we need to be conscious of, there are six skills which parents would do well to work on. Every parent knows that it requires a lot of skill to be a good mother or father. In fact, parenting skills are often developed along the way, through trial and error, and lots of practice. The following list of parenting skills can be a good starting point for the adventure of a lifetime called 'parenthood'.

- **Model Positive Behavior**
    It really is true that our children will, to a large extent, imitate what we do as parents. So if we want our child to be truthful, loving, responsible, sensitive and hardworking, then we had better be doing our best to be those things too. Words are very easy to say, but in the end it is our behavior that makes the most lasting impression.

- **Take Time to Listen**
    When we really take time to listen to our children we can learn so much. Not only about what is happening in their lives, but also about how they feel and what they might be struggling with. Try to sit down together at some point every day and allow your child to speak without interruption. Meal times or bedtimes are good opportunities for this.

- **Communicate Expectations Clearly**
    When you listen to your child, he will be more willing to listen to you. Clear communication is what it's all about, regardless of different parenting styles. When you are explaining your expectations, make sure your child understands exactly what you want and what the consequences would be if your expectations are not met.

- **Set Reasonable Boundaries**
    Children thrive when they know where the boundaries and limits are. However, if these are too restrictive or harsh, then the child may feel trapped and oppressed. This is where you need wisdom from God to find a happy balance where your child is safe but still has room to play and learn.

- **Be Consistent with Consequences**
    It is no use setting good boundaries if you are not going to enforce them. Every normal child needs to test those boundaries at least once to find out if you really meant what you said. By being firm and

consistent you will build trust and your child will learn to respect you.

- **Show Affection and Love Frequently**
  Of all the positive parenting skills, this is probably the most important. Make sure you hug your children every day and tell them how much you love them. When children receive frequent affection and affirmation, both physically and verbally, they will know they are loved and accepted. This will give them a strong foundation and confidence to face the world.

And finally a few last words before we close this chapter about bringing children into the circle of your marriage:

Parenting Requires Right Priorities...

For a Christian married person, the innermost circle of your heart is where Jesus Christ and your spouse belong, and every other relationship needs to shuffle up to another level. When your children come along, as precious as they are, they will need to go in the very next circle. Then close family members and friends and so forth. When these circles (or priorities) get mixed up and displaced it does not bode well for the marriage. For example, it often happens that children can slip into the inner circle and displace the spouse – this is bad news for both the marriage and the children. So if you are thinking that perhaps you and your spouse may be floating in different circles, it's time to do a little relationship stocktaking. Pray and ask God to help you set your priorities on track, getting the circles of happiness in your marriage in order again.

Questions for Reflection:

- When you hear the word "parenthood" what is the first thought that pops into your mind?
- Of the six aspects of conscious parenting, which one was most surprising or challenging to you? What is your response to this aspect – what actions will you take?

- Which of the six parenting skills do you feel you are handling pretty well? With which one would you like to up skill yourself?

Chapter 8: Waltzing Through Household Duties and Chores

Keeping things clean, tidy and running smoothly around the house can seem like a relentless task. And if you don't keep on top of it, in no time at all you will have piles and piles of dirty dishes and laundry, not to mention dust and grime. Then there's the cooking and gardening... and don't forget the bills that need to be paid too! Where do you start? Or rather when does it stop? If you and your spouse can relate to these kinds of sentiments, you are no doubt familiar with the repetitive routine of the Household Duty Waltz.

The Bible doesn't tell us exactly who should do what, but it does give some general guidelines saying that men should manage their household well (1 Timothy 3:12) and women should watch over the affairs of their household (Proverbs 31:27). As both husband and wife work together to keep their household in order it can be a wonderful labor of love (1 Thessalonians 1:3). With some careful planning, good communication and teamwork you could find yourselves waltzing gracefully through household duties and chores.

Here are a few tips and suggestions to help you handle the chores without getting into a war about it.

Forget about 50-50...

We have already mentioned this 50-50 myth in Chapter Four regarding conflict. There is no such thing as 'meeting halfway' in a marriage. If you are still counting and measuring then you need to stop and remember that when you got married it was a one hundred percent commitment. It's about doing everything you can, with all your heart, to help, bless, encourage and love your spouse. Of course this works best when both of you have the same mindsets, which is probably why you are reading this book because you want to have the best marriage possible. So getting back to the chores - yes, you both need to help lighten the load for each other, so that it is not an unbearable burden for just one of you. But it does not necessarily mean you will split the jobs exactly down the middle, which bring us to the next point.

Take your preferences into consideration...

We all have things we like doing better than other things. If you love cooking but your spouse can't stand it, and you hate washing dishes but they don't mind – then you have a win-win. If you both dislike cooking you will need to negotiate a roster where you both take turns. Try asking each other which chore you especially hate, and then as an act of love, you can be the one to do that chore in future so that your spouse doesn't have to – like you can do the laundry, while he does the sweeping or vacuuming. The same goes for the things you actually like doing, or the things you may be able to do better. Basically it's about communicating well and knowing each other's likes and dislikes, passions and expectations.

Know exactly what the chores are...

How many times have you thought, "Well, that's done now," and then you suddenly remember two or three more chores that still need doing? Running a household entails a whole host of duties and details, so it's a good idea at some stage to sit down with your spouse and make a list of everything from helping with homework, to buying birthday gifts and mowing the lawn. You might like to divide your list into daily, weekly, monthly or seasonal items. That way you can see exactly the extent of the work to be done and then figure out how best to cover all the bases. Once you have decided who will do what, release that person to do their job the way they feel it should be done. It's not going to work well if you are breathing down your spouse's neck and checking on all their jobs – rather just concentrate on yours.

Be flexible and sensitive...

If your spouse is not feeling well or has had a particularly difficult day, be ready to step in and take over his or her duties. And they would do the same for you when needed. It is good to reevaluate from time to time and maybe switch some things around for a change. Also the seasons of life may bring about changes in household demands, for example pregnancy, the arrival of children, sickness, extra commitments at work, or retirement.

Include your children...

Allocating chores to your children is an excellent and indeed vital learning opportunity for them. Start teaching your little ones from when they are tiny, and they will learn that housework is a normal part of everyday living. Young children usually respond well to star charts and they can enjoy the satisfaction and sense of accomplishment when their chores are ticked off. For older children or teenagers, one idea might be to have a family work hour where you all work at the same time to get the house straightened out. Then when it's done you can all relax together, instead of some working while others relax. Another lifelong benefit of teaching children to do housework is that when they have their own homes one day they will already be trained and ready to waltz through the housework with their future spouse (who will no doubt be very thankful).

Always express appreciation...

We all need encouragement and spurring on, especially when it comes to doing housework. A simple, "thanks for cooking a lovely meal," or a hug at the sink while you whisper, "thanks for washing the dishes" will go a very long way to lifting the spirits and lightning the load. And as you express your appreciation verbally and visually for your spouse, you will also be teaching your children to have thankful hearts. I Thessalonians 5:18 says, "give thanks in all circumstances, for this is God's will for you in Christ Jesus."

So at the end of the day, it's about teamwork. That means taking the attitude that this is our house so it is our work, rather than your jobs and my jobs. And as you cheerfully work together at keeping your house in order, you may just find yourselves gliding together in the waltz of household duties with the strength that God Himself gives you.

Questions for Reflection:
- What arrangement do you and your spouse presently have regarding the housework?

- Are you happy with the way things are, or would you like to see some changes? If so, what changes are you thinking of making?
- What can you do to foster a cheerful atmosphere of teamwork and servant-hood in your home?

Chapter 9: Balancing Marriage and Career

Marriage and career can sometimes feel like two opposite forces which threaten to pull you apart at times. Working long hours and overtime may seem unavoidable if you want to earn enough to provide for your family... but while you are working those long hours, you hardly get to see the spouse and family you are doing it for. It is not uncommon for parents to leave home while their children are still sleeping, and then return in the evening when it is almost bedtime again. Before you know it your children will be all grown up and you may have missed out on most of their childhood. More importantly, they will have missed out on having an involved parent. And your marriage will also suffer if you and your spouse hardly get time to connect deeply with each other.

The saying goes that no one on their death bed ever wished that they had spent more time at work, but regrets about lack of time spent with family are sadly rife. This part of the marriage dance can be particularly tricky, and if you don't learn to balance marriage and career, some painful consequences are inevitable. As Jesus said: "What good is it for a man to gain the whole world, yet forfeit his soul? Or what can a man give in exchange for his soul?"(Mark 8:36-37). In fact it is all about getting your priorities in order.

Ordering your priorities...

As a Christian, your first priority must be God, and then your spouse and your children. After that comes work, church and everything else. How you apply those priorities in your life will require a lot of wisdom, and constantly reminding yourself of who comes first, second and third. Thankfully God said if we lack wisdom we can ask Him and He will give it to us generously (James 1:5). You also need to bear in mind that different seasons in your life and marriage carry different requirements and demands. For instance, the early years when you are newly married will change dramatically when the babies start arriving. Then the next decade or so with young children in the home are bound to be particularly hectic, as well as the ensuing teenage years. Then comes college as your children reach young adulthood, before going on to marry and start families of their own. After that you have grandparenthood to look forward to with all the joys and challenges which that entails. As the Bible says, "There is a time for everything, and a season for every activity under heaven" (Ecclesiastes 3:1).

Working hard is good...

Jesus said that He came to give us life in abundance (John 10:10) and that includes the satisfaction of working hard and providing for our families. The Bible encourages us to be industrious like the ant (Proverbs 6:6-8) and in fact the Apostle Paul goes so far as to say that the person who does not work should not eat (2 Thessalonians 3:10). So working hard is good, but we need to do it with God's heart and attitude, not being sucked into the pattern of this world, but rather being transformed by the renewing of our minds as we offer ourselves to God (see Romans 12:1-2). In the work environment this may mean passing over a promotion if it means less and less time spent with your family. Or you may decide to relocate so that you can live nearer to your work and cut down on travelling time. You may be able to rearrange your work hours if your boss allows for flexi time, starting earlier so that you can get home earlier.

Keeping the rhythm of work and rest...

God never meant for you to work yourself to a standstill, that is why He instituted the Sabbath rest as a safeguard against exhaustion. It is essential to find a healthy rhythm between work and rest, on a daily, weekly, monthly and annual basis. With sufficient rest and relaxation, sleep and vacations, you can effectively pace yourself for the long haul. As much as possible try to set aside weekends for family time and recharging your batteries both physically and spiritually. One of the Ten Commandments God gave us is this: "Observe the Sabbath day by keeping it holy, as the LORD your God has commanded you. Six days you shall labor and do all your work, but the seventh day is a Sabbath to the Lord your God" (Deuteronomy 5:12-13).

Make mealtimes matter...

One part of a healthy daily rhythm is meal times. Everyone needs to eat, so why not make at least one mealtime per day a special occasion for your family to touch base and be together. Mornings are often rushed as you get ready for the day, but perhaps you could manage to hold hands and pray together before embarking on whatever the day may hold. Then in the evening, sitting around the dinner table together can be a valuable time to share your lives with one another as you enjoy the evening meal. Switch the TV off and just enjoy wholesome and hearty conversation. Ask each other about the highlights and lowlights of your day, and again take the time to pray and commit yourselves to God for the evening and night ahead.

Trusting God to provide...

Even while you are working hard and doing your utmost to provide for your family, it is important always to remember that in fact God is your provider. Matthew 6:31-33 reminds us that God knows what we need and if we seek His kingdom first He will add to us everything we need. Another wonderful promise is in Philippians 4:19 "My God shall meet all your needs according to His glorious riches in Christ Jesus." When King David was praising God in front of the whole assembly as they brought their gifts for building the temple, he said "Wealth and honor come from You; You are the ruler of all things. In Your hands are strength and power to exalt and give strength to all" (1 Chronicles 29:12)

Contentment is the key...

As you continue working faithfully and trusting God to provide for all your needs, you will discover the very precious and priceless treasure called contentment. The Bible says that Godliness with contentment is great gain, that as long as we have food and clothing we will be content with that. The Apostle Paul goes on to explain how the love of money is a root of all kinds of evil, and some who have been eager for money have wandered from the faith and pierced themselves with many griefs (1 Timothy 6:6-10). The key to contentment is placing God in the first place at the center of your life where He belongs, knowing that He is in charge and He will take care of you. You don't have to get everything done – only those things that God asks you to do, and leave the rest with Him. "Commit to the LORD whatever you do and your plans will succeed" (Proverbs 16:3).

Questions for Reflection:
- Do you feel that your priorities follow the order of God, then spouse, children, work, church and everything else? If not, ask God to show you what you can do to align them to His order.
- What do you do on a regular basis to relax and recharge your batteries?
- On a scale of one to ten how would you rate your "contentment quotient"? Make a commitment to consciously thank God for all His blessings and to be content with all that He provides for you.

Chapter 10: The Joy of Blessing Others

A blessing shared is a blessing multiplied. In the Christian life including Christian marriage, we are indeed blessed in order to be a blessing to others. When God called Abraham out of his homeland and told him to go to the Promised Land, God said "... I will bless you; I will make your name great, and you will be a blessing..." (Genesis 12:2). In Zechariah 8:13 God promises His people, "...I will save you, and you will be a blessing. Do not be afraid, but let your hands be strong." And in Hebrews 13:16 we are reminded, "do not forget to do good and to share with others, for with such sacrifices God is pleased."

Blessed to be a blessing...

In the land of Israel there are two seas; the Dead Sea and the Sea of Galilee. Both of these seas are fed by the River Jordan, but there is a huge difference between these two seas. The Sea of Galilee is vibrant and teeming with life; numerous species of fish, birds and lush vegetation abound. The Dead Sea however contains no life whatsoever as it is bitter and toxic, and no life can survive in its waters. How is this possible when they are both fed by the same source? The answer lies in the fact that the Sea of Galilee has both an inlet and an outlet, whereas the Dead Sea has only an inlet and no outlet. It only receives water from the Jordan River but does not pass it on.

And so it is the same with the living water of God's love and blessing which He pours into our hearts and lives so generously. If we pass it on to others we will experience His life and love more and more. One of the best contexts in which to pass on God's love is within the Church community.

Blessing in the Church community...

Meeting together regularly with other believers in a fellowship or church community is one of the greatest privileges. The Bible tells us that we are not to give up meeting together, but that we should encourage one another and consider how we may spur one another on toward love and good deeds (Hebrews 10:24-25). There is a very vivid metaphor comparing the Christian who is not part of a fellowship of believers as being like a coal which has rolled away from the fire – it will soon become cold and the fire in its heart will die. But if that coal remains close to all the other coals they will keep each other hot and burning brightly. The Apostle Paul describes the Church as the body of Christ, one body which is made up of many parts and each part has its unique role to play. As each one functions according to the gifts and talents they have received, the whole body is blessed (see 2 Corinthians 12:12-30)

Giving your children the gift of altruism...
One of the best gifts we can give our children is altruism: that is reaching out to others and making a positive contribution to alleviate the need, pain or suffering of someone else. Outreach can be one of the most bonding experiences for a family to do together. Whether it is making sandwiches to give the homeless, or donating toys and clothes to the less fortunate – there is always ample opportunity to give and to be a blessing to others. The younger we start the better; it is amazing how open and generous most children are when they are encouraged to give. As we give the gift of altruism to our children, this world will become a little better and they in turn will teach their children to do the same.

Opening your home to Friends...
Whether it's a camping trip, a day at the lake, or an evening playing board games, it's always more fun when some friends come along too. Encourage your children to invite their friends to join your family time. Perhaps those friends do not have stable homes and your family may be the only example they get to see of a happy, functional family. You will also be teaching your children to be inclusive rather than exclusive and to share their times of fun and laughter. It is certainly true that as you are a blessing to others, you yourself will be blessed in return. Proverbs 11:25 says, "a generous man will prosper; he who refreshes others will himself be refreshed."

In your marriage as you and your spouse seek to pass on to others the love and blessings that you have received from God, you will experience the deep joy of knowing that you were blessed to be a blessing, and that God is using you for His glory to bring thanks and honor to Him. And as you keep in step with the Master choreographer who is directing your marriage dance, He will lead you on and on in the beautiful and joyful dance of blessing others.

Questions for Reflection:
- In what ways have you and your spouse experienced the joy of giving in your marriage?
- If you have children, how are you encouraging them to become generous givers?
- Are you part of a Christian fellowship, and do you meet regularly with other believers?
- Read 2 Corinthians 9:8+11 out loud as a personal declaration as follows:

"... God is able to make all grace abound to me, so that in all things at all times, having all that I need, I will abound in every good work... I will be made rich in every way so that I can be generous on every occasion, and my generosity will result in thanksgiving to God."

Conclusion

Without a doubt most people would agree that marriage is more like a long distance marathon than a hundred meter sprint. Or to use the dance analogy, marriage is like an all night dance marathon, rather than one short dance sequence. It's all about the long haul, and it helps if you can hunker down, pace yourself and be prepared for whatever the years ahead may bring along.

The ages and stages of married life can be as different and distinct as the seasons, from winter to spring, summer and fall. First it's just the two of you, starry eyed honeymooners, still getting to know each other and figuring out how best to live together. Then you may decide to start a family and the next two decades will be filled with the demands of the baby, toddler, youngster and teenage years. After that they're off to college and work and you find yourselves alone together again. And by now a few gray hairs may be setting in, and then its retirement and the golden oldie years!

The question is how to keep your relationship healthy throughout all these different ages and stages of marriage? As this book has shown, the fundamental requirement of a good Christian marriage is having a real relationship with God, and placing Him at the center of your marriage. When Jesus is LORD of your life and when He comes first you can stay fresh as a couple and enjoy your special relationship, no matter what season or challenge you may be facing together.

Every living thing grows and changes over time, and it's no different with marriage. When your marriage relationship is alive and growing it will constantly be changing and developing. So you need to be flexible and re-evaluate as you go along. Your financial situation may change, you career or job may change, your family size may change as the children come along, you may face health challenges, or any number of other possibilities and circumstances. You can choose to see all of these changes as steps of growth and progress, asking God to teach you and give you His wisdom as you move along your journey of life together in marriage. As you stay flexible and adjust accordingly, you will help each other to stay fresh and healthy in your marriage, no matter what age or stage you are facing. As long as you face it together you will have many happy memories to share, and many thankful testimonies of God's goodness.

As you seek to learn the intricate steps of the magnificent marriage dance, only the Master Choreographer, God Almighty Himself can teach you correctly and excellently. As the creator and inventor of marriage, he is the One who knows what makes a happy and fulfilling marriage – one that brings joy to your heart and to the heart of God. So listen for His voice and read His love letter which He has given you in the Bible. He will tell you everything you need to know about marriage and life, so that you can enjoy the dance together with Him.

Before you go, would you please do me a favor? As an Independent Author and Self-Publisher, I don't have a large publishing company promoting my books. What I do have though, are reviews from readers like you. In fact, reviews are the single most important way for me to be able to get in front of more readers. Without them, I have no chance in competing with the larger, more established authors.

With that said, would you please go back and leave an honest review for this book? I would sincerely appreciate it.

Printed in Great Britain
by Amazon